WEST INDIES

Keith Lye
General Editor

Henry Pluckrose

Franklin Watts
London   New York   Sydney   Toronto

The Countries of the West Indies

Independent countries:
(with capital and in order of size)
Cuba (Havana)
Dominican Republic (Santo Domingo)
Haiti (Port-au-Prince)
Bahamas (Nassau)
Jamaica (Kingston)
Trinidad and Tobago (Port-of-Spain)
Dominica (Roseau)
St Lucia (Castries)
Antigua and Barbuda (St John's)
Barbados (Bridgetown)
St Vincent and the Grenadines (Kingstown)
Grenada (St George's)
St Christopher and Nevis (Basseterre)

Dependent countries:
Puerto Rico (US Commonwealth)
Guadeloupe (French)
Martinique (French)
Netherlands Antilles
Turks and Caicos Islands (British)
Virgin Islands (US)
Cayman Islands (British)
Virgin Islands (British)
Montserrat (British)
Anguilla (British)

Franklin Watts Limited
12a Golden Square
London W1

ISBN: UK Edition 0 86313 062 3
ISBN: US Edition 0 531 03762-2
Library of Congress Catalog Card No: 83-50110

© Franklin Watts Limited 1983

Typeset by Ace Filmsetting Ltd, Frome, Somerset
Printed in Hong Kong

Text Editor: Brenda Williams
Maps: Tony Payne
Design: Peter Benoist
Photographs: Zefa; Anne Bolt, 16, 17, 18; All Sport/Adrian Murrell, 21; Luke Hamilton, 30
Front Cover: Carnival time in the Bahamas (Zefa)
Back Cover: St Lucia (Luke Hamilton)

The West Indies are a chain of islands off the coasts of North and South America. The islands form a barrier between the Atlantic Ocean and the Caribbean Sea. Many islands, such as Marina Cay in the British Virgin Islands, are quite small.

The biggest island in the West Indies is Cuba, which is not far from Florida in the USA. The capital of Cuba is Havana. This modern city is the largest in the West Indies. About 1,900,000 people live there.

The explorer Christopher Columbus was captain of a Spanish ship when he discovered Cuba in 1492. The Spanish ruled Cuba until 1898 and two-thirds of the people who live there today are of Spanish descent. The rest are Blacks or are of mixed origin.

Cuba is a republic which is friendly with Russia. Portraits of Communist leaders are often to be seen, as here in the main square of Santa Clara, a town in central Cuba.

6

Cuba is famous for its cigars. Tobacco is an important crop in many West Indian islands. It grows well in the tropical climate.

This picture shows some stamps used in the West Indies. There are 13 independent countries in the West Indies. Britain, France, the Netherlands and the USA oversee the other islands.

Hispaniola is the second largest island in the West Indies. It has two countries: the Dominican Republic, where Spanish is spoken, and the Republic of Haiti, whose people speak French. This Roman Catholic cathedral is in Port-au-Prince, Haiti's capital. France ruled Haiti until 1804.

Women sell mangoes at a market in Port-au-Prince, Haiti. Most people in Haiti are Blacks. They are descended from Africans who were taken to the West Indies on slave ships hundreds of years ago.

Christopher Columbus was the first European to reach the West Indies. He landed in the Bahamas in October 1492 and his statue now stands in Nassau, the Bahamas' capital. Europeans quickly took control of the West Indian islands.

Fishermen sell shellfish from their boats at Nassau. Many West Indians fish to feed their families. They sell their catch locally. The only large ocean-fishing industry is in Cuba.

The sandy beaches of Montego Bay in Jamaica attract many tourists. Tourism is a major industry in the West Indies and over 500,000 visitors go to Jamaica every year. Jamaica lies south of Cuba. Its people speak English.

Farming is another leading industry in Jamaica. Bananas and sugar-cane are the main crops, for both grow well in a hot, humid climate. Women carry bananas to sell in the towns. Three-fourths of Jamaica's people are black.

15

Besides tourism and farming, Jamaica has an important mining industry. The chief mineral is bauxite, which is dug from the surface. The metal aluminium is made from bauxite. Jamaica is the world's third largest bauxite producer.

Puerto Rico lies east of Hispaniola. Modern buildings overlook the waterfront of its capital, San Juan. Puerto Rico is a self-governing Commonwealth of the USA. It has many powers of a US state. But its people cannot vote in US elections.

Children in Tortola, in the British Virgin Islands, learn how to use a microscope. West Indians take a keen interest in education. The Virgin Islands lie east of Puerto Rico and are split into two groups. Britain rules one group, and the USA the other.

Saint Croix is the largest of the US Virgin Islands. It has an oil refinery and other factories. The Virgin Islands are the group furthest north in the Leeward Island chain.

The Leeward Islands also include St Christopher and Nevis, a British Associated State until 1983. These children are lucky. Some West Indian children have no schools to go to.

Cricket is the chief sport on islands where English is spoken. The great cricket player Vivian Richards was born in the Leeward Islands, in Antigua. Antigua is a former British colony which became independent in 1981.

Sugar-cane is a major West Indian crop. This farm is in Guadeloupe in the Leeward Islands. Guadeloupe is a French Overseas Department.

The Windward Islands lie south of the Leeward Islands. They include Dominica, Grenada, Martinique, St Lucia and St Vincent. Young men in Grenada pick coconuts.

Martinique is a French Overseas Department, like Guadeloupe. In 1902, the volcano Mount Pelée (in the background) erupted with great fury. About 30,000 people in the coastal town of St Pierre were killed.

Like many West Indian islands, St Lucia was formed by volcanic eruptions. It has spectacular scenery. Formerly British, it became independent in 1979.

25

The islands of Trinidad and Tobago form a West Indian republic near South America. It is a major producer of oil. This refinery is near the capital, Port-of-Spain.

There is no water in Trinidad's Pitch Lake. Instead it is full of pitch (asphalt) which is used to pave roads. Pitch has been mined here since 1595, when the lake was first discovered by the English explorer Sir Walter Raleigh.

About one-third of Trinidad's people are of Asian descent. This village temple is used by Hindus. Trinidad's population is varied. Besides Asians there are also Blacks, a few Europeans, and others of mixed origin.

Fierce storms called hurricanes sometimes strike the West Indies. When this happens, crops may be ruined and people may starve. Here in St Lucia, boats have been hurled on to the land. The islanders work hard to repair the damage.

Tourism is the chief industry of Barbados, the island furthest east in the West Indies. Limbo dancers perform for tourists. They bend backwards to pass under a pole without touching it.

Everyone in the West Indies, rich or poor, loves a carnival. This mask is to be worn in a carnival in Trinidad. The West Indies are famous for music, singing and dancing.

Index

Antigua 21
Asphalt 28

Bahamas 12–13
Barbados 30
Bauxite 16

Carnivals 31
Columbus, Christopher 5, 12
Cricket 21
Cuba 4–7, 13

Education 18, 20

Farming 7, 15, 22–23
Fishing 13

Grenada 23
Guadeloupe 22

Haiti 8, 11
Havana 4
Hispaniola 8

Jamaica 14–16

Leeward Islands 19–22
Limbo dancing 30

Marina Cay 3
Martinique 24
Montego Bay 14
Mount Pelée 24

Nassau 12–13

Oil industry 19, 26

Pitch Lake 27
Port-au-Prince 8, 11
Puerto Rico 17

Richards, Vivian 21

St Croix 19
St Lucia 25, 29
San Juan 17
Santa Clara 6
Stamps 9

Tourism 14, 30
Trinidad and Tobago 26–28, 31

Virgin Islands 3, 18, 19

Windward Islands 23–25

J 972.9 L
Lye, Keith.   c.1
Take a trip to West Indies
                 8.90

DATE DUE

JAMES PRENDERGAST LIBRARY ASSOCIATION

JAMESTOWN, NEW YORK

Member Of

Chautauqua-Cattaraugus Library System